Spoken Words, Real Talk

by

Mimi Rose

ISBN: 978-1-917425-20-9

"I needed to write, to express myself through written language, not only so that others might hear me, but so that I could hear myself."

"The myth of normal"- Gabor Maté

Mimi Rose

Mimi has been a writer in a variety of ways. She has been songwriter, she is a playwright and has had two of her plays on in London, and one nominated for an off-west-end award. More recently, Mimi has been writing spoken word poetry. Mimi started to write when chronic illnesses took away her ability to do anything else. Writing is an outlet and expression which she can do when she's able to, and something that brings her a lot of joy.

Author's note

All my life I've loved words, hearing them, reading them, singing them. I suppose it was inevitable that I should end up writing them. I started writing when all my other choices were lost, due to chronic illness and disability.

At a milestone birthday, I realised that I had a lot to say as myself, as opposed to fictional characters. I wanted to take an honest look at a life lived so far, as a Black first-generation woman, living with chronic illnesses and disability. I had more to say than even I realised.

Last summer, as I sat outside in my garden for 30 minutes each day, chasing the sun, nature took over. It freed my mind, and I wrote emotive and genuine words about race, racism, chronic illness and disability, motherhood, the world today and healing from trauma.

These words were in turn sometimes poignant, sad, funny, genuine, powerful, angry and life affirming for me. I hope these words make you feel seen, feel vindicated, heard, comforted, entertained, and yes even laugh at times.

Best Wishes,
Mimi x

CONTENTS

Disrespect

Musical Suggestion-
"Golden" Jill Scott

*I wrote this after yet another micro-aggression,
except it never feels that micro...*

How?

How many?

How many times?

How many times can...?

How many times can I?

How many times can I allow?

How many times can I allow it?

No more times tomorrow, ever, again.

No more times tomorrow, ever.

No more times today.

No more times.

No more.

No.

Eyes Unseen

Musical Suggestion-
"I wish I knew how it would feel to be free"
Nina Simone

*I wrote this piece after hearing about a young
Black gymnast in Ireland, who was overlooked
when it came to handing out the prizes.*

Where is my prize?
Where is my medal?
Our eyes are meeting, her eyes blue, mine
brown.
Her eyes look away to the next blue-eyed person.
She gets my medal.

I stand alone, the only one without a prize.
I smile, I don't make a fuss,
so that I might be remembered.
Because maybe, she's just forgotten.
More eyes meet mine; they tell me to smile.

I do, but no prize still, just... a photo.

Inside I feel sad I worked so hard
But my brown-eyed gymnast skills are not
enough here.
Inside, my eyes are crying, outside my eyes still
smile.

She looks down the aisle the blue-eyed one.
One more medal left, it must be mine.
The eyes look down and find me.
It's too late, it's time to go.
No audience claps for me.

We leave the arena, a medal is placed quickly
around my neck, a rub of the head, and a gentle
push forward
say, it's the end.

I still don't cry.

Even The Machinery...

Musical Suggestion-

"Moanin'" Art Blakely and The Jazz Messengers

"Our findings demonstrate that people from most ethnic minority groups have experienced greater rates of death involving COVID-19 compared with people of White British background during the pandemic" - ONS (Office for National Statistics - 2021)

There's a machine, a lifesaving machine,
that measures our oxygen levels accurately.
Well not mine, but some of us.

Not the global majorities' oxygen levels, some of us.
That machine is 3 times more likely to show readings,
wrong readings, because of our skin tone.

You see it was never tested on all of us, when
developed.
How is that possible? We are the global majority.
Should it not have been tested globally?

The machine dictates who will get oxygen,
who will be admitted for oxygen,
who will be transferred to ITU for oxygen.
The machine is lifesaving,
but whose life, is it saving?

The Medical Race

Musical Suggestion-
"Rockit" Herbie Hancock (45 seconds in)

"Black patients with melanoma have an estimated five-year melanoma survival rate of 71 percent, versus 94 percent for white patients... Skin cancer represents 1 to 2 percent of all cancers in Black people." *The Skin Cancer Foundation.*

You can't have that, that's not for you.
That's a rare condition, not for you.
We can't test for that, not for you.
You can't have that.

How about hypertension, no? with a side order of diabetes?
Yes, you can have that.
What about high BMI? Or BPD or what? What's that you're saying?

Oh no, we can't have that, no aggression, be
grateful, be accepting.

You have symptoms I can't see, no sorry I can't
see that rash,
I can't see that lump; I can't see that you wince
when you walk.
I can't see that the oxygen saturation is wrong,
wrong skin tone for accuracy.
It could cause death, but that's just how it goes
sometimes.

I can't hear you; I don't understand when you
speak to me.
You speak well, how come?
Pain on a scale of nine out of ten, have this
paracetamol, they'll do the trick.
That's not enough, but your pain threshold is so
high, no need for more, you'll be fine.

You may be dying, you may be seriously ill, you
may be having debilitating side-effects.
But what's your blood-pressure doing?
Keep taking the medicine for it, you'll be fine,
until you're not.
And if you're not, well you're BMI was high.

Di Foolish
(In Jamaican Patois)

Musical Suggestion-

"Dubbing in the Dark" Dennis Bovell & Joe Ariwa

Supremacy comes in all colours.

A kill dem want fi kill we?

A dat dem want?

All de time dem a chat racist idea from dem

mout.

All dem times, dem seh, a too much a we.

Dem seh, a we cause crime, it black on black.

But no mention wen it, white onna white,

Or just white.

A silence dem wan fi silence we?

A dat dem want?

Shh, yuh nuh fi complain or mention de

treatment.

Be grateful and accept.

Yuh nuh fi mention it,
Just smile, de masked smile,
Wey hide de hurt.
But dem nuh care, causin, we a smile
And all a dis come from de top.
Dem seh, what dem global minority colleagues,
cannot say.

A fool dem wan fi fool we?
A nuh we a di fool.
Wen di Brown and Black children of immigrants
Demself seh, that immigrants nuh good,
Dat dem mus guh back, weh dem come from,
Stop cause all di problem.
But dem did hav problem before we arrive
Dat's why we were invited.

Di Black and Brown people, di confused ones in
power
Will seh anyting, for the de power.
Even if, a demselves dem a imprison.
But the people dat dem want fi impress, a go turn
pon dem one day.

Dem can't fool wi, dem just tink dem can.

Dem can't silence wi, dem just tink dem can.

We must learn bout we history, where we come
from.

B.E, Before Enslavement.

Dis is our history, after that, is white history
month every day.

We invented, we created, we had riches.

We had medicines, and science and architecture,
and books and engineering,
long before di res of the world.

Den dem come and traffic wi, fi dem own
purpose, History interrupted, fi wi history.

Dem can't kill that history, nuh matter how hard
dem try, we can't allow it,

We nah allo it, it no go suh.

Two Worlds

Musical Suggestions-

"Gypsy" Fleetwood Mac (English World)

"Stir it up" Bob Marley (Jamaican World)

I wrote this in English and Jamaican patois to show the two worlds.

I'm a first-generation British Jamaican, or is it second?

Some say first, others say second.

My parents... Jamaican, so, what it does it matter?

All my life, living in two worlds.

Jamaican inside the house, English outside.

Yu fi learn yu book, hav mannahs, a who yu a chat to like dat?

Yu tink mi and yu is fren?

Those who cannot here, mus feel.

Come, eat yu dinner, yu wash yu han first?

Whey yu mean tea? A propa dinner, dis.
Yes, cornbeef, and rice and cabbage, come, nuh
mek it get coal.
Whey yu did have fi lunch today?
Spam? What is dat?

School: other children boast of homework, not
done.
Boast of shouting at parents or slamming doors.
Describe, visiting their nans and grandads,
And having cake and sandwiches for dinner, or is
it tea?
Talk about free time, no jobs, no chores, no
cleaning.
No staring, no name calling, no spitting at, no
abuse.

But wen we guh home, loud music a play pon di
gram,
It a come out a di good front room.
Visitahs is here.
Di food smell good, chicken, and rice and peas,
Mmmm sweet potato puddin.

Di parents dem happy, dem a smile

Dem a laugh, dem a dance.

We dance too.

Di tree bar heater is on

Di room feel warm

And everting, nice!!

The Colour of Supremacy

Musical Suggestion-
"War" Bob Marley

*How must it feel to suddenly be in the middle of
a war?*

You're minding your own business, and then you
hear a loud explosive sound. You don't know why.
But other's do...
They want something you live on, live with or are
surrounded by.
They want it, apparently, they need it, and now
you cannot live with any normality.
In fact, your normality is over.

Everything you value is in tatters, not even basics
of life are accessible now.
You have an eviction notice on your life, it will
never expire and may lead to death.
It's not personal, it's not about you.

They will make it personal, and about you.
It will be manufactured, created, rivalries
enhanced or created, battles enhanced or
created.
And whilst that rages, by stealth they will take it,
all.
All the gas, all the oil, all the cobalt, all the
lithium, all the bauxite, all of it.

And you may be displaced, your infrastructure
will be destroyed.
Your life is expendable.
Your life does not have the value of others.
Apparently, others deserve more...
Others, are more deserving,
Apparently.

Tek Tek

Musical Suggestion-

"Police and Thieves" Junior Murvin.

*I wrote this after I read about people
fighting "David and Goliath" battles against
multi-millionaire land grabbers in the Caribbean.*

A tek dem want fi tek.

Dem tek wi from wi land.

Dem put wi somewhere else.

Dem lef wi.

Den dem come back fi more.

Now dem want di land.

Dem want di beach.

Dem want all a it, fi dem pleasure.

A nuh time fi dem lef wi alone?

    ... In Peace.

The riches here, a fi wi.

Shop close, stealing time, dun.

Tribute to Black Women

Musical Suggestion-
"Everything is everything" Lauryn Hill

There are so many things and so many occasions that inspired this piece, but what finally made me write this, was when Diane Abbott M.P. stood up 43 times in the Houses of Parliament to try and ask a question, and was ignored, 43 times. Especially when they were talking about her, and the racist threat to her life. Now she is the "Mother of the House", we rise.

We are not here just to survive.
We're here, we're present, we're courageous.
We're not going anywhere.
We're powerful, we're creative
We're not going anywhere.
We're beautiful, we're sexy,
We're not going anywhere.

We are here to take up space.

We are here to be our full authentic selves.

Stand to your full height, spread out your arms,

Fill the space, we are here to be.

We are here to rise.

We are here to thrive.

We are here to love ourselves.

We are here to recognise the beautiful queens

within us.

The beauty of our skin,

the wonderment of our hair.

The joyfulness of our spirit,

The playfulness of our souls,

The generosity of our psyche,

The power of our minds,

The sheer amazing awe of us.

We are not here just to survive.

We are here to thrive.

Rise up, lift up your arms to the sun,

Hold up your head,

Take up space, we are free to be.

We are not here just to survive

We are here to thrive

Rise up, lift up your arms to the sun,

Hold up your head,

Take up space, I am free, you are free, we are

free…to be.

Rage

Musical Suggestion-
"In da club" Josh Vietti

After an unhelpful appointment
with a hospital consultant that I had been
waiting for, for a long time ...

I have rage, unlimited, hidden, unfiltered rage.
It's there all the time.
Sometimes in disguise, sometimes so obvious it
burns.
It burns my insides; it makes my cells vibrate at
the wrong frequency.
The frequency is set at irritations, at frustrations,
at sadness, at hatred.
I hate the health care professionals who have
colluded, contributed, and creatively kept me in
illness, when healing would do. When all they
had to do was:

Listen.

All they had to do was work as a team.
But no, they systematically dissect me.
Not heart, Cardiology, not liver, Hepatology, not
Pancreas, Gastroenterology, Neurology,
Psychology.
All the ologies added together with the wrong
values, with incorrect assumptions, means the
answer is wrong.

It's always wrong.

So now let's turn on the patient.
They are now angrily responding, it's your fault,
you did something wrong.
You omitted or added or mixed in something, and
now you're sick.

It's you, it's all you.

Nothing to cure here because it's all in your brain.

You imaginatively created your own special illness.

But don't worry they've even got an ology for that too.

And they successfully, or unsuccessfully try to shunt you into that space of

Oblivion.

If I go willingly, they've won, another one off the books, if I resist, well it's proof that I'm more ill than they thought.

And still the rage continues.

Clues ignored, big and small.

Lies are told, big and small.

Whatever fits the narrative.

But... I'm still in there, still worth fighting for.

Until the rage is replaced, until the healing is

Complete.

SuperPowers

Musical Suggestion-
"Rooted in the earth" Sound effects zone

Sometimes we just don't realise
how amazing we are.

This was inspired by living with a condition called MCAS- (Mast Cell Activation Syndrome), but could easily be applied to living with any long-term illness or disability)

Super- Power, an exceptional ability or extraordinary power.
We have a remarkable super-power to survive, every day, despite it all, whether we like it or not, whether we want it or not.
Every day we discover new ways, and old ways, and amazingly creative ways we never imagined.

Because, every day is a triumph of survival, and
every day, when the clock clicks past midnight,
we've done it again.

No one knows, unless they know us personally,
and sometimes even they don't know, how we do
it, most of the time, neither do we.
We are the "canaries in the coal mine ",
the sensitive ones,
the ones who know first,
the ones whose bodies are so alert,
changes signal on a cellular level, every day.

And so, we have to find, new ways:
New ways to eat,
New ways to wash,
New ways to socialize,
New ways to take medication,
New ways to travel,
New ways to be, every hour, every minute, every
second of our lives.

It's a heavy burden to carry, and yes, we could really do without it.

BUT

We are incredible body detectives.
We are awesome survivalists.
We are unbelievably resilient.
We are incredible problem solvers.
We are truly, amazing, and these, are our super-powers.

Yeah

Musical Suggestion-
"Lay Down" Son Little

*When you realise just how exhausting it is
to fight for good healthcare every day.*

Ok, I give up, I surrender, yeah whatever you
want.
Yeah, I'll take that medicine, yeah, I'll suffer those
side-effects.
Even though I feel disgustingly bad.
Yeah, I'll ignore those symptoms.
Yeah, I'll believe they're all in my head if that's
what you need.
Yeah, I'll deny rationality and logic, if that's what
you need.
Yeah, I'll ignore the obvious, and try not to
investigate anything, if that's what you need.

Yeah, I won't connect the dots, I'll take your word
for everything, even when my instincts are
screaming at me... that's wrong.
Yeah, I won't explore any complimentary
treatments if that's what you need.

Yeah, I'll accept everything you say as gospel, if
that's what you need.
All the fight, all the heart, all the instincts, all the
common sense has been drained out of me
today.

Now, just a nodding shell of myself, with an air of
begrudging compliance, I don't feel better, but
you do.
Is this what you want? Yeah?

Knowing

Musical Suggestion-
"Keep Going" This is the Kit

Yet another rubbish hospital appointment!!
Misogynoir perhaps?

Who knows me better than me? No one
Who feels my feelings better than me? No one
Who understands me better than me? No one.
Who gets it? I do.

I do know whether the symptom is new or old.
I do know whether it's worse, or better.
I do know something about the illness, I live it, do
you?
I am an expert in me, my condition, medications,
treatments, side effects, triggers.
Who lives with it? I do.

So, I meet you, it's been a long time coming.

The anticipation has built up like a weird blind date.

Are you going to be <u>kind?</u>

Are you going to be a <u>good</u> listener?

Are you going to <u>really</u> see me?

Are you going to <u>believe</u> me?

On rare occasions, it's a match, I feel seen, success!!

Otherwise:

I quickly realise I've arrived at Gaslighting Central, but I'm prepared, I'm ready.

"It's all here, look", I show them, they decline.

Tell me in your own words, these are my own words.

Their words, deny, accuse, belittle, misunderstand, sometimes actually, lie.

So, I start to feel helpless, angry, subdued, mystified as to what just happened.

It's another day, at the Doctors.

You've given the wrong answers, sorry, and just like a game show contestant, it's time to leave, so the next contestant can come in and try their luck, on the 'It's all in your head' gameshow.

Don't go in there, I want to whisper, as we cross paths, me coming out, you going in, the game is rigged.

Today I feel tired

Musical Suggestion-
Theme from "Hill Street Blues"
Mike Post, Larry Carlton

Today, I'm tired. I'm tired of trying to do the right thing.
I'm tired of being so bloody positive.
I'm tired of trying to arrange my day, so it's just like what I assume, everyone else's is like.
I'm tired of pretending a purpose I just don't feel today.

I'm tired of smiling when inside, I'm crying. I'm tired of the loss, after grieving, after everything.
I'm tired of new symptoms, old symptoms, of, for god's sake what now? symptoms.

I'm tired of feeling scared. Scared to allow the negative in, just in case, I never feel positive again. In case I scare all the people away, until even I can't stand to be in the same room as myself, imagine!!

But, what if, I let go.

What if I dare, not to try, and hold it all together, to mask how I really feel, both physically and mentally.
What if, I try not to be smiling, and oh so positive, but to be questioning, why? There is no clear answer, I know that. It's just I really, really want to know. Knowing won't necessarily help, I'll still feel ill, still be ill.
So maybe, just for today, I should allow myself to be, how I genuinely feel. And just maybe, this will allow a brighter future tomorrow. We all deserve a day off, right?

Guess what, 24 hours later… it did, today, I feel better, not cured, but better.

Burnt out

Musical Suggestion-
"Try a little tenderness" Otis Redding

She thought she had to be perfect, you see.

She thought, she had to be everything that was good.

She thought, she had to achieve more and more endlessly.

She thought, it would bring her joy.

But the joy just kept moving.

The goal posts just kept shifting.

The people just kept expecting.

The mind just kept whirring.

The whirring in her mind stopped her thinking, about what she really wanted, about what she really needed.

I mean, would she have chosen all those things?

Would she have chosen to do them all, at the
same time?

At the time, yes, she thought constantly, moved
constantly, did constantly.
Saying yes until exhaustion, was what she chose.
Look at me, I'm doing it all, I'm being it all, I'm
amazing.
Can't you see?

But they didn't see when it was too much.
They didn't see that she was beside herself with a
longing for rest.
That wanted to be, that wanted to feel, free.
Now, she has more time, time that has been
imposed,

She's almost grateful.
She thought she had to be perfect, you see.

The One

Musical Suggestion-
"Optimistic" Sounds of Blackness

*A long song for such a short poem, it's worth
listening until at least 1min 55 secs though.*

Yesterday I met the one.
The one who listened, with empathy.
The one who asked me about my opinions and
choices and took them on board.
The one who said don't worry, I see you, I hear
you.
The one who melted my anxieties.
The one who cared.
It was a doctor, and my heart sang.

Wishing

Musical Suggestion-
"Cruisin'" Smokey Robinson

You never know what you've got... until it's gone.

When it was 2019
Life was great.
If only I'd known.
I wish I'd learned to appreciate the freedom I
had.
I wish I'd learned to appreciate.
I wish for

When it was 2019
Life was great.
If only I could have known.
I wish I'd learned to appreciate freedom.
I wish I'd learned to appreciate.
I'm wishing for

When it was 2019

Life was great.

If only I'd known that it was all about to end.

I wish I'd learned to appreciate all the freedoms.

I wish I'd learned to appreciate.

I wish.

The Longing

Musical Suggestion-
"This woman's work" Kate Bush

There it is again.

A sharp pain, that makes you wince,

it catches, then it's gone.

It is hard to identify where it is exactly.

Is it the mind, body or soul?

The pain comes when you experience, the

longing.

You can't talk about the longing.

It's not socially acceptable or logical.

After all you've been successful.

It's what's supposed to happen.

You are pleased and proud.

It's ok, you've done your job well.

So why the longing?

Fetal cells migrate to the mother during
pregnancy.
And can last for decades, and in the brain forever.
So, we can literally carry our children within us,
for decades, forever and always.
So, when they leave us, when they develop lives
independent of us,
through action, distance, or both.
Maybe, that is why the longing can just descend
upon us.
We have no control over it.

And sometimes we fight it, because it defies
logic.
Afterall it was always the plan, right?
Mothers, respectfully, and lovingly, allow it, if you
feel it.
It is part of who we are, part of mothering, part
of life.

Betrayal

Musical Suggestion-
"Tadow" Machego, FKJ

You think you know people.

You think you know a group of people.

You think you're safe.

They seem… nice.

One day you realise that niceness, is not as it

seems.

That niceness is conditional.

One day you realise, that what you thought you

knew, was wrong.

Because the mask slipped,

Not just a little bit.

The mask slipped right off.

There was no time to catch it, or quickly readjust.

Anger, ego and indignation pushed it right off.

And then it was the naked rage, entitlement, and

more ego.

Loud words, uncivil words, sweary words, harsh words.

Faces contorted, expressions disfigured, atmosphere destroyed.

All around, everyone feels the fallout.

Stomachs clench, breaths are held, bodies are frozen.

No one knows what just happened.

Everything stops... for a minute.

It's like being on the top of a roller coaster... before the rapid descent.

Before, the scary anticipation.

Do I dare look? Only through my fingers.

Can I cope with the next bit?

It feels so terrifying, but you have to go anyway.

You have no choice; you have no agency.

Down you go, powerless, except, it's not, a thrill.

Illusions

Musical Suggestion-
"Liar Liar Ge2017" Captain Ska

Governments, eh?

They're lying to you, can't you see?
Every day lying.
They lie about health, they lie about money, they
lie about immigration,
they lie about water safety, they lie.
It's what they do.
It's what they're good at.

They must protect their way of life at all costs.
Your way of life, your very existence is
completely, expendable.
You're just a number, a percentage point, a mere
decimal point of life.
They keep you worried, stressed and sick even
though they could do something to help.

So much so, that you can't see what's being done.

So, you're not aware.

They disconnect you from others with lies, with misinformation that creates divisions.

So, you can't feel connected and safer.

They flood your world with misconceptions, misinformation, and bots from farms to tell you maybe want you what to hear, but not the truth.

And all the time they get richer, they stay healthier, they have a better standard of life, and you? What about you?

Quiet Desperation

Musical Suggestion-
"Patriot's Cello" Third World, Cat Coore

Shh!!

We are living lives of quiet desperation.

It's not the same anymore.

Every day is a series of knots we tie ourselves in,

as we try to convince ourselves otherwise.

But the knots aren't secure.

Our well-hidden truths loosen them and then we

panic,

Because how will we hold it altogether without

them.

We are living lives of quiet desperation.

It isn't the same anymore.

2019 is becoming a distant memory, we can

never return to.

Because how can we, now there's a scar, where
the world was,
and the healing is only surface.
Below the surface is the word we do not name.
A new 'c' word, that is now more offensive that
the other one.

We are living lives of quiet desperation.
It can't be the same anymore.
New illnesses, weird illnesses, sudden deaths,
short illnesses, foggy brains, poor memories.
And it doesn't respect age.

Some people seem… different, less patience, less
tolerance, less care,
No allowances made for you.
It's just them grappling alone.
To stay healthy, or return to 'normal', or just live
<u>their</u> lives,

But the spectre of 'C' lives amongst them still, it
never went away.
Allergies, summer colds that last, summer flu,
strange viruses, 100-day coughs.
'C' In disguise maybe?

We are living lives of quiet desperation.
It won't be the same anymore.
Because the rich and the powerful, got richer,
and more powerful,
from the suffering, and their shares in PPI,
vaccines, funeral homes and care homes.

For inside their, secretly masking, hepa-filtering,
PCR tested worlds, it's not the same, it's much
better.
They don't get 'ill' repeatedly, they stay well,
alive, safer.
Why aren't we angry at them, and not each
other,
when we mask, or filter, to keep safe, and well
and alive.

We are living lives of quiet desperation,
Can it ever be the same anymore?
Who knows?
When we can no longer hide from the quiet
voices, that tell us that, this isn't right.

When we can no longer outrun the research.
When we can no longer unsee the evidence right
in front of us.
When the knots we tie ourselves in finally all fall
away.
What will we do then?

Time Stealers

Musical Suggestion-
"Time" Hans Zimmer

Is time moving faster and faster?
Or, are we at the mercy of… The Time Stealers!!!

Those activities that quietly steal our time,
sometimes good things, sometimes bad, but
mostly, very definitely, annoying.
Like talking to phone companies, listening to
phone menus.
Being put on hold and hearing the same irritating
track for ages,
Looking for your phone, how much time is taken
by these?

Fixing unexpected computer issues, waiting for
the bloody blue circle to stop spinning.

Proving you're not an actual robot. I mean what
the hell! Those photos, sometimes, you just don't
<u>see</u>, the last set of traffic lights.

Calling to complain versus calling to buy, the
same company, completely different time scales.
Trying to find the actual contact number in the
first place, in its well-hidden spot.

Waiting for your card to be approved, have you
noticed how card readers are always... glitchy.

Trying to call the doctor for an appointment, at
8.30 a.m. "you are number 27 in the queue", and
when you do get through, "All our appointments
are gone".

How come it takes so long to find anything to
watch? I mean the algorithm is set up for you.
Bad boxsets, good box sets they're all, leaching
your time.

Waiting: Waiting for repairs, plumbers, electricians, builders, deliveries, whole mornings, afternoons or evenings drift by.

Creating new passwords, for everything all the time. Oh, you don't like that one, can't use that character, or number, not that symbol, oh for god's sake. Then, how long trying to remember them, months later, yep it's time to create a new one, and the process stats again.

Booking anything online; flights, concerts, holidays, several pages later you get to the payment page, then you've got to prove it's you, which is good security. "Please log into the app on your phone", but where is your phone?

The Time-Stealers are at it again.

What Kind of World?

Musical Suggestion-
"That's the way of the world"
Earth, Wind and Fire

In 2020 I was designated "vulnerable".
In 2022 "vulnerability" is officially over.
I wish someone had told my body.

What kind of world are we living in?
Denial, Denial, Denial.

For if we deny, it cannot exist, except it does.
There is a global pandemic. Shh, don't mention
the 'C' word, not that one, not the four-letter
word, that's rude. The five letter one, it also
starts with 'C', but ends in 'D', shall we call it CD?
CD came into the world and has changed it
forever. CD exposed us to a virus, a deadly,
debilitating virus and it never left.

It exposed our humanity, our relationships with
nature, the environment, our relationships with
each other. It highlighted, kindness,
connectedness, an end to societal inequality.
It created a resurgence of creativity, of new ways,
of different priorities, of greater awareness of
racial disparities.

But then it also exposed the realities of capitalism
and patriarchy and white supremacy. We can't
have people realising that throughout an illness
or because of it, there's a new way to be.

And so, it was changed, CD is officially over they
said, it's done, time now to get back to reality.
And so mass denial was spawned, nurtured, and
grown into a fully-fledged adult.

So many sick people with their symptoms, but we
now call it flu, in the summer? So many times?
Bad colds, unusual infections, sudden deaths,
deaths after a short illness of all ages, long C, M.E
anything but CD.

No more masks, no more mitigation, just people dying for clean air. But not the rich, or the movers and shakers of the world, as they live and work in their secret clean air, multiple PCR tested worlds. Because if you tell the people every day the lie, the lie becomes fact.

Numbers

Musical Suggestion-

"54-46 was my number" Toots & The Maytals

1.Numbers

   2. Have

      3. Always

         4. Been

            5. Numbering.

Who decides the numbers that we live our lives by?

Are they experts, what are their names?

Who decided that 10,000 steps is the right number?

Someone did.

Then someone created apps, dedicated to informing us, reminding us, recording us, and downright bullying us to do the 10,000 steps or else?

We become programmed, we must do it, or else
we have to make an appointment with the failure
part of our brain.
Where, we are shamed and told to try harder
tomorrow.

Exercise is good for us, but why 10, 000, why not
9,500 or 10,250.

What about BMI?
It is your judge, and it decides your character as
well as your health, only a lazy and greedy person
would have a high BMI, and be deemed obese,
when looking like a stick.
Strive to lower it, you may now look and feel
unhealthy, but the numbers, say you are now…
a success.

Favourable poll results, achievement targets at work, BOGOF, followers on social media, likes on social media, ratings, marks out of ten.

How would we know how to feel without them? How do we do we know what to do without them?

Questions

Musical Suggestion-
"God gave me feet for Dancing"
Ezra Collective, Yasmin Lacey

What if we knew how our lives would end, when
it began?
How would that change the way we live it?

Would we pace ourselves?
Would we still rush to try and complete
prescribed life goals, before a certain age?
Career, job, house, kids, marriage before 30? Or
not?
Would we strive to become our best selves?
Or would we say, sod it? And do what we want.

Would we have children later, or not at all?
Would we eat healthily and exercise three times a
week?

Would we be hedonistic, and do it all, good and
bad?
Would we be kind to our fellow humans and the
environment?

Would we treat it like a race or a journey?
Would we live for the now?
Would we try to sensibly have savings and a
pension?
Would it make us ask more questions, or less?

A Return

Musical Suggestion-
"Sha La La (Make me happy)" Al Green

What is courage?

Is it facing your fear?

How can you face it when you can't see it?

Is it behind you, or beside you, or in front of you?

Should you feel the fear? Or ignore the fear?

Should you push it down, eat it or drink it?

Should you express the fear?

If you feel scared, or anxious, who do you tell?

You don't want them to feel it too.

You don't want to spread it like some contagious
disease.

You don't want to seem vulnerable, be…
vulnerable.

But you are, and that's good, isn't it?

You're human, and you yearn for things, and life
and experiences.

But each of these can be terrifying, especially after a long... pause.

You are awakening, as if you've been asleep for a long time.

You are finding a new you, or a well-hidden old you.

A forgotten you, rediscovered.

You like her, she is both familiar and new.

Is she scared? A bit, but that's ok.

She is feeling the gift, she has given to herself... courage.

Better

Musical Suggestion-
"Fly me to the moon (In other words)" Bobby
Womack

What will you do when I'm better?

Will you throw me a party?

Will you bake me a cake?

Will you smile? Will it reach your eyes?

Will you laugh and sing with me?

Will you laugh out loud with gratitude?

Will you be full of joyfulness?

Will you be happy for me?

Will your soul be relieved?

Or, will you wonder about your place in the
world?

In my world.

Garden

Musical Suggestion-

"Outside my Window" Stevie Wonder

Sitting in my garden, some might call it
overgrown- wondering.
How to fix it, and make it look acceptable-
thinking.
Acceptable to who? – asking.
Then the sun shines, and the warmth arrives –
realising.
There is beauty in imperfection, you just have to
be patient.

Through the weeds, there's beautiful colours,
Through the leaves are a thousand shades of
gorgeous greens.
Bees buzz loudly, they see the beauty, depend on
it.
Butterflies weave in and out and adorn it some
more.

Birds settle for a while and layer the soundtrack with their songs.

There is beauty in imperfection, we just have to look... with patience.

The art of saying 'no'

Musical Suggestion-

"NO" Megan Trainor

"NO!"

Hope

Musical Suggestion-
"Hello Sunshine" Aretha Franklin

I went outside and waited…

for the sun,

it…

arrived…

beautifully.

Happiness

Musical Suggestion-
"Boogie Oogie Oogie" A Taste of Honey

My happiness was right there.
I realised once I rediscovered it amongst all the other stuff.

My happiness isn't dependent on people, places, money or even health.
My happiness is a state of mind and body.
My happiness is a feeling that bubbles up inside me and resets the dial of emotions to joy.

It was underneath, hidden by expectations of what I should have.
Assumptions of what others appear to have.
Revelations of what society dictates I need or must have.

Predictions of what I should have achieved, at my age.
Survival mechanisms I adopted to achieve it all, and still be...

Now, I've learned to let it all go, the assumptions, revelations, predictions, and survival techniques.

I'm letting go, and like a helium balloon in the sky, they're getting further and further away.

Now, the bubbles of joy are rising higher within me, and filling me with calm, peace and healing. I greet them,

"Hello" I'm glad you came.

Playlist for "Spoken Words, Real Talk"

1. "Golden" Jill Scott
2. "I wish I knew how it would feel to free" Nina Simone
3. **"Moanin'"** Art Blakely and The Jazz Messengers
4. "Rockit" Herbie Hancock (45 seconds in onwards)
5. "Dubbing in the Dark" Dennis Bovell & Joe Ariwa
6. "Gypsy" Fleetwood Mac (English World)
7. "Stir it up" Bob Marley (Jamaican World)
8. "War" Bob Marley
9. "Police and Thieves" Junior Murvin
10. "Everything is everything" Lauren Hill
11. "In da club" Josh Vietti
12. "Rooted in the earth" Sound Effects Zone
13. "Prana" Nu Meditation Music
14. "Keep going" This is the Kit
15. Theme from "Hill Street Blues" Mike Post, Larry Carlton
16. "Try a little tenderness" Otis Redding

17. "Optimistic" Sounds of Blackness

18. "Crusin" Smoky Robinson

19. "This Woman's Work" Kate Bush

20. "Tadow" Machego, FKJ

21. "Liar Liar Ge 2017" Captain Ska

22. "Patriots Cello" Third World, Cat Coore

23. "Time" Hans Zimmer

24. "That's the way of the world" Earth, Wind and Fire

25. "54- 46" was my number" Toots and the Maytals

26. "God gave me feet for dancing" Ezra collective, Yasmin Lacey

27. "Sha la la (Make me happy) Al Green

28. "Fly me to the moon" Bobby Womack

29. "Outside my window" Stevie Wonder

30. "NO" Megan Trainer

31. "Hello Sunshine" Aretha Franklin

32. "Boogie Oogie Oogie – A Taste of Honey

Below is a QR code which will take you directly to the playlist on Spotify.

(For those like me who are technically challenged, open your cameras, point at the image below, and click on the link that appears).

www.ingramcontent.com/pod-product-compliance
Lightning Source LLC
Chambersburg PA
CBHW061041050726
47592CB00004B/1543